Who Grows Up in the Desert?

A Book About
Desert Animals
and Their Offspring

Written by Theresa Longenecker
Illustrated by Melissa Carpenter

Content Advisor: Julie Dunlap, Ph.D.
Reading Advisor: Lauren A. Liang, M.A.
Literacy Education, University of Minnesota
Minneapolis, Minnesota

PICTURE WINDOW BOOKS
Minneapolis, Minnesota

Editor: Peggy Henrikson
Designer: Melissa Voda
Page production: The Design Lab
The illustrations in this book were prepared digitally.

Picture Window Books
5115 Excelsior Boulevard
Suite 232
Minneapolis, MN 55416
1-877-845-8392
www.picturewindowbooks.com

Printed in the United States of America.

Library of Congress Cataloging-in-Publication Data
Longenecker, Theresa, 1955–
  Who grows up in the desert? : a book about desert animals and their offspring / written by Theresa
Longenecker ; illustrated by Melissa Carpenter.
    p. cm.
  Summary: Describes animal babies found in the desert, including young desert pocket mice, roadrunners,
Gila monsters, and more.
  ISBN 1-4048-0024-7 (lib. bdg. : alk. paper)
  1. Desert animals—Infancy—Juvenile literature. [1. Desert animals. 2. Animals—Infancy.]
I. Carpenter, Melissa, ill. II. Title.
  QL116 .L66 2003
  591.3'9—dc21
                                                                                            2002006287

Deserts are harsh, dry places. The sun-baked ground can burn your bare feet. The cool night air can make you shiver. Many baby animals grow up in the desert. Some need help from their parents, while others grow up quickly and take care of themselves.

Let's read about some baby animals that grow up in the desert.

Kit

A baby fennec fox is called a kit.

Kits stay cool in an underground home. A few weeks after birth, the kits are ready to leave their home, or burrow. They go with their mother to hunt for insects, mice, and lizards.

Did you know?
At birth, a fennec fox kit is smaller than a child's fist. The kit's eyes are closed, and its big ears are folded flat against its tiny head.

Chick

A baby roadrunner is called a chick.

Roadrunners can't fly very well, but they can run fast. Soon these chicks will be running across the sand. They can catch their own food when they are less than one month old.

Foal

A baby Arabian camel is called a foal.

A camel foal is born with strong legs. It can walk just a few hours after it is born. The foal will stay close to its mother for up to two years.

Did you know?
Like its parents, the foal has long eyelashes. These lashes keep sand out of the camel's eyes.

Hatchling

A baby sidewinder rattlesnake is called a hatchling.

Once sidewinder hatchlings are born, they are on their own. As they grow, their skin falls off, or sheds. Underneath is a new, bigger skin. Hatchlings will shed their skin six or seven times by their first birthday.

Did you know?
A sidewinder hatchling is born with no rattle. Each time the snake sheds its skin, some dead skin is left at the end of its tail. This dead skin forms one ring of the rattle.

Pinkie

A baby desert pocket mouse is called a pinkie.

At night, pinkies snuggle up in an underground nest. Their mother is out looking for seeds to eat. A pinkie's first food is its mother's milk. As soon as a pinkie can eat seeds, it will leave the litter and live on its own.

Did you know?
A pinkie is born with no hair and pink skin. By the time the pinkie leaves its nest, it has grown hair and is beginning to look like its mother.

Pup

A baby dingo is called a pup.

Newborn dingo pups drink their mother's milk. As they grow, the mother chews and swallows food, and then coughs it up for the pups to eat. When the pups are a few months old, they learn to hunt.

Did you know?
Both the mother and father help raise the pups. The pups will stay with their parents for almost one year.

Hatchling

A baby Gila monster is called a hatchling.

A Gila monster hatchling uses its special egg tooth to cut open its eggshell from the inside. After leaving the shell, the hatchling goes looking for bird eggs and small animals to eat. This baby is already a fierce fighter.

Scorpion young

Baby scorpions are called scorpion young.

Scorpion young hang on to their mother's back with their tiny pincers. After a week or two, their soft baby shells peel off. Underneath are bigger, tougher shells. Once the scorpion young have tough shells, they can leave their mother and live on their own.

Fast Facts

Fennec Fox: Fennec fox kits drink their mother's milk for a few weeks after they are born. Then they begin to hunt and look for berries, leaves, and roots to eat. Most of the foxes' water comes from their food. Fennec foxes have the smallest bodies of all foxes—and the biggest ears! Those big ears help keep the foxes cool. Body heat escapes from the thin skin on their ears.

Roadrunner: Roadrunner chicks get attention from both their mother and father—even before they hatch. At night, the father takes his turn sitting on the eggs. His body stays warmer through the cool nights than the mother's. A roadrunner is one of the few animals that eat rattlesnakes. The bird is so fast, it can catch the snake before it bites.

Arabian Camel: The Arabian camel has one hump on its back. The camel's body stores fat there. That way, the camel can go a long time without eating. A camel foal hasn't eaten enough yet to make a lot of fat. Its hump is still small. But its feet are already quite big. A camel's foot has two toes that spread out when it steps down. This broad, flat foot keeps the camel from sinking into the shifting sand as it walks.

Sidewinder Rattlesnake: At birth, hatchlings are six to eight inches (15 to 20 centimeters) long. As many as 18 hatchlings are born in a litter. They hatch from eggs inside the mother's body. Once born, hatchlings find their own food. Sidewinders eat mice, lizards, and other small animals. Sidewinders hunt at night. During the heat of the day, they rest in the shade of a rock or bury themselves in the sand.

Desert Pocket Mouse: Pocket mouse pinkies are born and raised in underground burrows with several rooms, or chambers. A litter usually has about four pinkies. Pocket mice get their name from the fur-lined pockets on the outside of their cheeks. They carry seeds in these handy pockets.

Dingo: Dingoes live in the deserts of Australia. Pups are born in a shady den. Up to four or five pups might be born in a litter. Dingoes live together in packs, the way wolves do. A pack includes the parents, the pups, and often a few other adults. Dingoes hunt rabbits, small kangaroos, and wild pigs.

Gila Monster: A Gila (HEE-luh) monster hatchling stays inside its eggshell for a few days after hatching. The hatchling soaks up the rest of the egg yolk and drinks the liquid in the egg. After it leaves the nest, the hatchling hunts for food during the cool desert nights. Gila monsters are cold-blooded. This means that their body temperature goes up and down with the air temperature around them. During the day, they rest so they won't get too hot. Gila monsters are one of only two kinds of poisonous lizards.

Scorpion: Scorpion young hatch from eggs inside the mother's body and are born 25 to 35 at a time. As they are born, the young fall onto the mother's folded legs. Then they climb onto her back. A sting from a scorpion's tail can kill insects and other small animals.

Desert Babies at a Glance

Word for Baby	Animal	Born How	First Food	Word for Female	Word for Male	Word for Group
Kit	Fennec fox	Live	Mother's milk	Vixen	Reynard	Leash
Chick	Roadrunner	Egg	Insects, small lizards	Female	Male	——
Foal	Arabian camel	Live	Mother's milk	Mare	Stallion	Herd
Hatchling	Sidewinder	Live*	Small animals	Female	Male	——
Pinkie	Pocket mouse	Live	Mother's milk	Female	Male	——
Pup	Dingo	Live	Mother's milk	Female	Dog	——
Hatchling	Gila monster	Egg	Eggs, insects	Female	Male	——
Young	Scorpion	Live*	Insects, spiders	Female	Male	——

* Eggs hatch inside mother.

Where Do They Live?

Fennec fox — northern Africa

Roadrunner — southwestern United States and northern Mexico

Arabian camel — northern Africa and the Middle East

Sidewinder rattlesnake — southwestern United States and northern Mexico

Desert pocket mouse — southwestern United States and northern Mexico

Dingo — Australia

Gila monster — southwestern United States

Scorpion (about 1,300 kinds!) — deserts of the world as well as other areas

Match the Animal with Its Fact

Trace a line with your finger between the question on the left and its answer on the right.

Questions	Baby Animals
Which newborn babies have big ears folded flat?	Scorpion young
Which babies run fast across the sand?	Desert pocket mouse pinkies
Which babies ride on their mother's back?	Fennec fox kits
Which babies are fierce little fighters?	Arabian camel foals
Which babies eat food their mother coughs up?	Sidewinder hatchlings
Which babies have long eyelashes?	Roadrunner chicks
Which babies shed their skins many times?	Gila monster hatchlings
Which babies look for seeds to eat as soon as they leave their underground nest?	Dingo pups

Words to Know

burrow — a hole or tunnel in the ground made by an animal, usually for its home

cold-blooded — having a body temperature that goes up and down with the air temperature

den — a wild animal's home, usually a shallow hole or cave

litter — a group of animals born at the same time to the same mother

lizard — an animal with four legs, a long tail, and small pieces of hard skin called scales on its body

pincer — a hard claw that can open and close to grab things

poisonous — having a substance that can hurt or kill something

shed — to drop or fall off

To Learn More

At the Library

Baker, Alan. *The Desert.* New York: P. Bedrick Books, 2000.

Butterfield, Moira. *Animals in Hot Places.* Austin, Tex.: Raintree Steck-Vaughn, 1999.

Gray, Susan Heinrichs. *Deserts.* Minneapolis: Compass Point Books, 2001.

Martin, James. *Poisonous Lizards: Gila Monsters and Mexican Beaded Lizards.* Mankato, Minn.: Capstone Press, 1995.

Fact Hound

Fact Hound offers a safe, fun way to find Web sites related to this book. All of the sites on Fact Hound have been researched by our staff. *http://www.facthound.com*

1. Visit the Fact Hound home page.

2. Enter a search word related to this book, or type in this special code: 1404800247.

3. Click the FETCH IT button.

Your trusty Fact Hound will fetch the best sites for you!

Index